Becoming Her
The Journey Through Womanhood

"She thought she had to be everything to everyone — until she remembered she was already enough."

Vgdawson

Books on Friendship, Relationships, and Personal Growth

Books on Personal Growth and Life Reflection

The Love Dilemma: Staying with the one you love

I need to think about my life choices

Books on Relationships and Personal Boundaries

My Best Friend

The Friendship Years

Books for Readers Life After 50

The Truth about the Golden Years: What Aging Really Reveals

Discover More

Visit the author online for additional books, resources, and inspiration: **www.what2buynext.com**

Published by
Second Season Press
Birmingham, Alabama
www.what2buynext.com
ISBN: 978-1-972518-15-1

Cataloging information is available from the Library of Congress.
Library of Congress Control Number: 2026912484
First Edition: 2026

This book is a work of nonfiction. The information presented is based on the author's experiences and research and is intended for educational and informational purposes only. The author and publisher disclaim any liability for any injury, damage, or loss resulting from the use of the information contained herein. Readers are encouraged to seek professional guidance when appropriate.
All brand names and product names referenced in this book are trademarks or registered trademarks of their respective owners. Their use is for identification purposes only and does not imply endorsement.

Printed in the United States of America

Disclaimer

This book is written for inspirational, reflective, and personal growth purposes only. The stories shared within are drawn from real experiences, observations, and composite narratives to represent the emotional truths many women face throughout different stages of life.

The author is not a licensed therapist or counselor, and the content in this book should not be taken as professional mental health, legal, or medical advice. Readers are encouraged to seek professional guidance for emotional, psychological, or relational issues that require individual attention.

This book is intended to uplift, heal, and provide perspective — not to judge or diagnose. Every reader's journey is unique, and healing takes time, courage, and compassion.

This book is dedicated to every woman who has ever loved deeply, carried silently, and kept going when no one noticed.

To the **daughters** who tried their best to be what their parents needed — even when it meant losing pieces of themselves.

 To the **sisters** who loved through rivalry, who stayed connected through tears and distance, and who never stopped showing up.

To the **friends** who were always the listeners, the healers, and the ones who gave without being asked.

To the **wives** who carried the weight of love, loyalty, and sacrifice — and found their strength in the quiet moments of rediscovery.

To the **mothers** who loved when love hurt, prayed when faith wavered, and held their children in heart even when distance grew.

To the **grandmothers** who became the keepers of wisdom, teaching us that grace is the truest form of love.

And to the **woman herself**, who, after everyone else was cared for, remembered to finally care for herself.

May you find yourself in these pages, and may they remind you that you were never just one role, you were Becoming Her all along.

With love,

Vgdawson

Womanhood is one of the most beautiful and emotionally complex journeys a person can experience. It is filled with seasons of joy, sacrifice, heartbreak, endurance, reinvention, and quiet strength that often goes unseen by the world.

I wrote *Becoming Her* because I believe many women spend their lives caring for everyone else while rarely stopping long enough to ask themselves:

"How did I get here?"

"Who am I beneath all these responsibilities?"

"When do I begin living for myself too?"

This book was born from observation, lived experience, conversations, reflection, and the emotional truths women carry silently every day. Some stories in these pages may feel familiar. Some may feel deeply personal. Others may remind you of women you have loved throughout your own life.

My goal was never to create a perfect image of womanhood. Instead, I wanted to honor the real experience of it — the complicated, emotional, exhausting, beautiful process of becoming.

This is a book about women who kept going while carrying sorrow nobody else fully understood. It is about learning that failure, disappointment, motherhood struggles, broken relationships, loneliness, and emotional exhaustion do not define a woman's worth.

Most of all, this is a book about rediscovery.

Because no matter how many roles a woman has carried, no matter how much of herself she gave away through the years, there is still time to return to herself again.

I hope these pages make women feel:

seen,

understood,

comforted,

and less alone.

Thank you for allowing me to walk beside you on this journey.

With love,

Vgdawson

Table of Contents

What readers are saying!

Here's what readers are saying about the works of vgdawson:

"Her writing feels like a conversation with a lifelong friend —

raw, honest, and full of wisdom."

— Reader Review, I Need to Think About My Life

Choices

"Every page feels like therapy for the soul. I saw myself in her

words and felt seen for the first time."

— Reader Review, Friends for Life

"Vgdawson's books always meet me where I am — broken,

hopeful, and ready to begin again."

— Reader Review, Dear Self: Reflections and

Resilience Across Life's Journey

"She writes about womanhood with grace and truth. It's as if

she's lived every story she tells — because she has."

— Book Blogger Review

Becoming Her: The Journey Through Womanhood is an emotional and reflective exploration of the many roles women carry throughout life — and the personal identity they often struggle to hold onto along the way.

Inside these pages, you will journey through:

he expectations placed on daughters,

the complicated bonds between sisters,

the beauty and heartbreak of friendship,

the emotional realities of marriage,

the deep sacrifices of motherhood,

the exhaustion of single parenting,

the wisdom of grandmotherhood,

and the rediscovery of the woman herself.

This book is written in a compassionate, conversational style — like siting across from someone who understands the quiet things women often carry but rarely speak aloud.

You can expect:

heartfelt storytelling,

emotionally honest reflections,

real-life inspired examples,

wisdom rooted in lived experience,

and gentle encouragement toward healing and growth.

This is not a book that judges women for their struggles or

choices. It is a book that honors the emotional complexity of

womanhood with grace, empathy, and truth.

Some chapters may make you smile in recognition.

Others may bring tears.

Some may help you understand yourself — or the women in

your life — more deeply than before.

Above all, this book is meant to remind you of one important

truth:

you are not behind,

you are not ruined,

and you are not too late.

You are still becoming.

Introduction

There are moments in every woman's life when she stops and wonders; how did I get here?

Not just the physical here, but the emotional one. The space between who she used to be and who she has become. The world calls it growing up, maturing, or evolving; but to many of us, it feels like becoming.

Becoming the daughter who carried her family's hopes.
Becoming the sister who held everything together.
Becoming the friend who gave until she was empty.
Becoming the wife who stayed when love grew quiet.
Becoming the mother who loved past exhaustion.
Becoming the grandmother who learned forgiveness.
And finally, becoming the woman herself, the one who survived it all.

This book was born from years of reflection from listening to women's stories and seeing the strength behind their tears. It is a mirror held up to the generations before us and a hand extended to the women walking beside us now.

You will not find judgment here. Only truth. Only empathy. Only the kind of love that understands what it means to live for others and then find your way back to yourself. Becoming Her is a journey through the phases of womanhood; not to glorify perfection, but to honor the beauty in imperfection. To remind every woman that even when life didn't turn out the way she planned, she still has the power to rewrite her story with grace, wisdom, and dignity.

So, before you begin, take a deep breath.

This is your story too, in one way or another. And no matter what chapter of womanhood you find yourself in today, remember this:

You are still becoming.

— Vgdawson

Chapter 1: The Daughter: Born into Expectation

From the moment a daughter takes her first breath, she inherits a silent contract, one she never signed, but one written long before she arrived. It's an unspoken agreement of duty, obedience, and perfection. She is taught to smile even when she's unsure, to keep her voice soft but her grades high, to make her parents proud no matter what it costs her. The world tells her that being "a good girl" is the highest honor, yet no one explains the weight that comes with trying to be everything to everyone.

For many daughters, love and approval become intertwined. We chase validation not because we don't know our worth, but because we were told love must be earned through good behavior and sacrifice. We learn to measure our success not by joy but by how happy others are with us. Somewhere in that equation, our true selves quietly fade into the background.

The Girl Who Never Disappointed

Ava grew up in a home where perfection was praised and emotions were inconvenient. Her mother, a woman of strong faith and structure, believed that success was a reflection of good parenting. Ava learned early that mistakes were unacceptable. She studied hard, spoke softly, and never challenged authority. Every compliment from her parents became another link in the chain of who she thought she had to be.

By her teenage years, Ava had mastered the art of being "the good daughter." But beneath the polite smiles and perfect report cards, she was suffocating. She hid her anxiety behind achievements and her exhaustion behind compliance. When she finally left for college, she thought she was free; yet she still heard her mother's voice in her head, judging every choice.

It wasn't until years later, as an adult and mother herself, that Ava realized she had never truly known what she wanted. Her entire identity had been shaped by what her parents expected her to become. The hardest truth to accept was that the love she chased as a child had already been hers; she just didn't know how to believe it without earning it.

Ava's story is not one of rebellion, but of awakening. The quiet kind. The kind where a woman finally understands that being loved does not mean being perfect.

The Daughter Who Chose Herself

Lena was the opposite of her older sister; bold, outspoken, and unwilling to live by anyone's rules. Her mother often compared the two, calling Lena the "wild one." But what her mother saw as rebellion was actually self-preservation. Lena refused to live under the shadow of expectation.

When she left home at eighteen to pursue art instead of medicine, her parents cut her off financially. "You're making a mistake," her father said, disappointment heavy in his voice.

And maybe she did. There were years of struggle, jobs that barely paid rent, and nights she cried from loneliness. But they were her mistakes. Her tears. Her life.

Years later, when her art began to gain recognition, her parents attended one of her exhibitions.

Her mother stood before a painting titled Unfinished Love, a portrait of a young woman reaching for her mother's hand, only to find it fading. "Is this me?" she asked. Lena simply nodded.

In that moment, they both understood the cost of unmet expectations; not just the distance between them, but the years lost in silence. Forgiveness didn't happen overnight, but it started that day. Because love, when it's real, always finds its way back home.

The Good Daughter Syndrome

There is a quiet pressure many daughters carry long before they understand what pressure even is. It begins subtly — in the tone of a parent's voice, in the praise given for being "good," "helpful," "mature," or "responsible." Before long, the little girl learns something dangerous: love feels safest when she performs well.

So she becomes the good daughter.

She learns not to complain too much.

Not to cry too loudly.

Not to ask for too much.

Not to become a burden.

And while others may see her as mature for her age, what they often fail to notice is that maturity born too early usually comes from survival, not peace.

Some daughters become emotional caretakers before they even become teenagers. They sit quietly beside exhausted mothers, absorb tension during arguments, help raise younger siblings, or become the child everyone "depends on." While other children are discovering who they are, these daughters are learning how to manage everyone else's emotions.

The tragedy is not that they became strong.

The tragedy is that many of them never learned they were allowed to be soft too.

For years, they continue carrying that role into adulthood. They become women who over-give, over-explain, overachieve, and overextend themselves trying to earn the approval they never fully felt. They struggle with boundaries because somewhere deep inside, they still fear disappointing someone.

The little girl inside them is still asking:

Did I do enough to be loved?

The Daughter Who Grew Up Too Fast

Monica was only sixteen when her mother became ill.

Overnight, childhood disappeared. She woke up each morning making breakfast for her younger brothers, making sure homework was done, helping with bills, and trying to hold the household together while still attending school.

Teachers praised her maturity. Family members called her "such a strong young lady." But no one asked Monica how heavy it felt carrying responsibilities that were never meant for a child.

She stopped thinking about college after graduation because her family needed help financially. Instead, she found a full-time job and convinced herself she was doing the right thing.

Years later, Monica sat in her car outside a grocery store and cried after seeing a group of college students laughing together. It wasn't jealousy exactly. It was grief. Grief for the version of herself she never got to become.

She whispered something painful that day:

"I spent my whole life taking care of everyone else before I ever learned how to take care of myself."

Many women quietly carry this same sorrow. They do not resent helping their families. What hurts is realizing nobody noticed what it cost them.

The Invisible Burden of Being "The Responsible One"

Families often lean hardest on the daughter who appears the strongest. She becomes the dependable one. The fixer. The peacemaker. The child who "never gives problems."

But strength can become a prison when nobody remembers you need care too.

Many daughters become women who feel guilty resting. Guilty saying no. Guilty choosing themselves. Even happiness can feel uncomfortable because they were conditioned to believe their value came from sacrifice.

This emotional pattern shows up everywhere:

- in relationships where they over-function,
- in friendships where they carry emotional weight,
- in careers where they burn themselves out,
- and in motherhood, where they attempt perfection because failure feels unsafe.

What began in childhood quietly follows them for decades.

And the hardest part?

Many women don't even realize they are still living as that little girl seeking approval.

The Daughter Who Could Never Say No

Angela's mother often reminded her, "Family comes first." It sounded loving growing up, but over time, Angela noticed it always came with expectations.

She was the daughter everyone called when something went wrong:

- babysiting nieces and nephews,
- loaning money,
- helping relatives move,
- siting in hospitals,
- solving family conflicts.

At first, she felt honored to be needed. But by her late forties, she was exhausted. Her own dreams had been postponed so many times she barely remembered what they were.

One evening, her daughter asked her a question that shook her deeply:

"Mom, what do *you* enjoy doing?"

Angela froze.

Not because she didn't know the answer — but because nobody had asked her that in years. Including herself.

That question forced her to confront a painful truth: she had spent so much time becoming useful that she forgot how to simply become herself.

When Approval Becomes Identity

One of the greatest emotional struggles daughters face is confusing approval with love.

Some women grow into adulthood believing:

- if they work harder, they'll finally feel worthy,

- if they sacrifice enough, they'll finally be appreciated,

- if they never disappoint anyone, they'll finally feel secure.

But approval is temporary.
Real love does not require exhaustion as proof.

Healing begins when a woman realizes she no longer has to earn her place in people's hearts by abandoning herself.

That realization changes everything.

Because eventually, every daughter must answer a dificult question:
Who am I when I stop trying to become who everyone else expects me to be?

What This Season Teaches Us

The daughter phase of life shapes the emotional foundation

many women carry forever. It teaches us how we see ourselves,

how we receive love, and whether we believe our needs

matter.

Some daughters were nurtured gently.

Others were shaped through survival.

Most were a combination of both.

But no matter how childhood unfolded, every woman deserves

the opportunity to separate her identity from her obligations.

You are not valuable only because you are responsible.

You are not lovable only because you sacrifice.

And you are not selfish for wanting peace, rest, or joy for

yourself.

At some point, every woman must stop asking:

"What do they need from me?"

And begin asking:

"What do I need from myself?"

Because becoming her begins the moment a daughter realizes

she deserves care too.

A Mother's Reflection

Every daughter carries the echo of her mother's voice; the one that tells her who she should be, how she should act, what she should sacrifice. But eventually, every woman must decide whose voice she'll listen to from that moment on.

Being a daughter isn't about obedience; it's about becoming.

And sometimes, the greatest act of love toward your parents is to live your truth, even when they don't understand it.

We are all someone's daughter; molded, shaped, and sometimes wounded by the people who raised us. Yet womanhood begins the moment we stop seeking permission to exist as ourselves.

The Daughter: Born into Expectation

"Some daughters spend their entire lives trying to become the woman they think will finally make everyone proud."

Chapter 2 – The Sister: Silent Rivalries and Unspoken Love

Sisterhood is one of the most complex bonds a woman will ever know. It's both love and rivalry, devotion and distance, laughter and tears; all wrapped inside one lifelong connection.

Sisters grow up under the same roof but often in different worlds. One might live in the light of approval, while the other fights for acknowledgment in the shadows. What parents often mistake for sibling rivalry is sometimes a daughter's quiet plea to be seen.

The truth is, sisterhood teaches us early about comparison; about how easily love can feel conditional, how quickly it can turn into competition.

But it also teaches us forgiveness, resilience, and the unspoken language of loyalty that survives even when words fail.

The Shadowed Sister

Naomi was the second-born; the quiet one, the one who never caused trouble. Her older sister, Camille, was radiant: class president, homecoming queen, her parents' pride and joy.

Naomi adored her sister, but she also envied her. Every time her mother praised Camille, Naomi felt herself shrink a little more.

When they were young, Camille often defended Naomi from teasing at school. But as they grew older, the distance between them widened.

Camille moved away, married young, and lived the life their parents always wanted. Naomi stayed behind, caring for their aging mother, puting her own dreams on hold.

Years later, when their mother passed, Camille came home for the funeral. Naomi, tired and unspoken for so long, finally broke the silence. "You got to live your life," she said softly. "I stayed and lived hers." Camille didn't respond, not out of indifference, but out of guilt.

It took years, and many quiet visits, for the sisters to find their way back to each other. Not through apologies, but through understanding. Naomi learned that comparison had stolen their closeness, and Camille learned that success without connection is an empty victory.

When they finally sat side by side, older now, the silence that once divided them became a peace that bound them.

The Sister Who Became the Mother When life shifts, sisters often become each other's saving grace. That was the case for

Renee and Mariah. Their mother passed when Renee was eighteen, and Mariah was only twelve.
In a moment, Renee went from sister to caregiver.

She promised her mother she'd take care of Mariah no matter what. But promises made in grief are heavy ones. Renee worked two jobs, attended night school, and gave up her social life to raise her sister.

Mariah resented the rules, never understanding that Renee's strictness came from fear; fear of failing the promise she made to a dying mother.

The years between them were filled with slammed doors, silent dinners, and tears cried in separate rooms. But time has a way of softening pain. When Mariah became a mother herself, she finally saw what her sister had carried alone.

"I used to think you were trying to control me," Mariah said one night, holding her newborn. "But now I know you were just trying to keep me from breaking."

Renee smiled through tears. "I was still learning how not to break myself."

Their love didn't erase the years of misunderstanding, but it transformed them. It became a story of resilience, where duty turned into devotion, and regret became gratitude.

The Quiet Lessons of Sisterhood

Being a sister is a lifelong education in love's complexity. It teaches patience, comparison, forgiveness, and endurance.

Some sisters walk together through every phase of life; others drift apart and find each other again only in old age. Yet even in distance, there is a thread that never truly breaks.

We may not say it often enough, but every sister carries a piece of the other; the laughter of childhood, the scars of arguments, the shared memories of where they came from.

If womanhood begins with the expectations of our parents, then sisterhood becomes our first mirror; reflecting both who we are and who we're trying to become. And sometimes, it's that reflection that teaches us the truest meaning of compassion.

Sisters Who Become Strangers

There is a unique heartbreak that comes when sisters drift apart. Unlike friendships that fade naturally over time, the distance between sisters carries history with it — childhood memories, shared pain, family secrets, old wounds, and the silent understanding that no matter how far apart life pulls them, they are still connected by blood.

Yet some sisters become strangers while still alive.

Sometimes it happens slowly:

one gets married and moves away,

one becomes the caretaker for aging parents,

one feels overlooked,

one feels judged,

one carries resentment the other never even realized existed.

And before long, birthdays become short phone calls. Holidays become uncomfortable gatherings filled with polite conversation instead of closeness.

The saddest part is that many sisters still love each other deeply even while carrying unresolved hurt. Pride often becomes the wall standing between reconciliation and healing.

As girls, sisters may fight over clothes, attention, or personality differences. But as women, the conflicts become heavier:

money,

caregiving responsibilities,

inheritance,

parenting differences,

emotional wounds from childhood.

Some sisters spend years silently competing with one another without ever admitting it. One sister may appear more successful, more loved, more financially stable, or more emotionally secure. The comparison becomes exhausting, even though neither woman fully understands the burdens the other carries privately.

The truth is this:

Every sister is fighting a battle the other cannot completely see.

The Sister Who Stayed Behind

Carolyn and Denise were only two years apart growing up, but their lives unfolded very differently. Denise left their small hometown, went to college, traveled, and built a successful career. Carolyn stayed home, cared for their aging mother, worked two jobs, and raised her children nearby.

At family gatherings, people constantly praised Denise's accomplishments while quietly assuming Carolyn had "settled." What no one understood was how much Carolyn had sacrificed for the family.

Over time, resentment grew silently between them. Denise believed Carolyn judged her for leaving. Carolyn believed Denise abandoned the family responsibilities she was left carrying alone.

Years passed with surface-level conversations and emotional distance, nor one knew how to fix.

Then their mother passed away.

After the funeral, Carolyn finally broke down and said the words she had held inside for years:

"You got to become yourself. I became what everybody needed."

Denise wept immediately because for the first time, she truly understood her sister's pain.

That night, the two women sat together for hours talking honestly — not as competitors, but as tired women who had both carried different kinds of sorrow.

Healing didn't erase the past, but it softened it.

And sometimes, that is enough.

The Sister Who Knows Your Beginning

A sister remembers versions of you nobody else does. She remembers:

who got blamed more,

who cried easily,

who tried hardest,

who felt invisible,

who protected whom,

who carried the tension in the household.

These memories shape relationships long into adulthood.

Some sisters become each other's safest place. Others become reminders of unresolved childhood wounds. And sometimes they become both at once.

There are sisters who:

stop speaking for years,

reconnect after illness,

become closer after losing parents,

or finally forgive each other once age softens pride.

Time has a way of changing perspective.

As women grow older, many realize the arguments that once felt enormous were often rooted in pain, insecurity, or misunderstanding. Aging teaches sisters something important: Life moves quickly, and love matters more than being right.

Two Sisters Find Their Way Back

Vanessa and Renee had not spoken in almost twelve years. What started as a disagreement over money after their father's death slowly turned into bitterness, silence, and family division. Holidays became awkward. Their children barely knew each other.

Both women secretly missed the relationship they once had, but neither knew how to bridge the distance after so much time had passed.

Then Renee became ill unexpectedly.

When Vanessa heard the news, she sat in her car for nearly an hour debating whether to visit. Pride told her to stay away.

Love told her to go.

She went.

The moment she walked into the hospital room, Renee burst into tears. Not because the past suddenly disappeared — but because illness stripped away everything unimportant.

The sisters talked honestly for the first time in years:

about grief,

about jealousy,

about feeling abandoned,

about expectations and neither one knew how to carry.

And somewhere between those painful truths, they found each other again.

Not perfectly.

But genuinely.

Sometimes healing between sisters does not come through grand apologies. Sometimes it comes through simply deciding: "I don't want to lose more time."

Aging Changes Sisterhood

There is something deeply tender about watching sisters age together.

The same girls who once fought over bathrooms and borrowed clothes eventually become women discussing medications, caring for aging parents, worrying about grown children, and grieving the people they've lost.

The competition fades.

The urgency softens.

And what remains is history.

Many women eventually realize their sisters are among the few people who truly understand where they came from emotionally.

Even imperfect sisterhood carries a bond that is dificult to explain.

Because sisters are often witnesses to one another's becoming:

the dreams,

the heartbreaks,

the mistakes,

the resilience,

and the survival.

And sometimes, simply being witnessed by someone who remembers your beginning is its own form of love.

What This Season Teaches Us

Sisterhood teaches women some of life's earliest lessons about love, comparison, forgiveness, and identity.

It teaches us:

how deeply words can wound,

how silence can create distance,

and how love can survive even complicated history.

Not every sister relationship is easy. Some women grow up best friends with their sisters. Others spend years longing for closeness that never fully came.

But one truth remains:

family relationships are rarely simple because they carry generations of emotion beneath them.

As women grow older, many begin to understand that healing does not always require perfect agreement. Sometimes it simply requires compassion — the willingness to see each other as human beings shaped by the same storms differently.

And perhaps one of the greatest gifts sisters can give one another is this:

the freedom to stop competing and simply belong to each
other again.

The Sister: Silent Rivalries and Unspoken Love

"Sisters know the oldest version of who you are — the one that existed before the world touched you."

Chapter 3: The Friend: The One Who Listens but Is Rarely Heard

Friendship is where we first learn the meaning of chosen love; the kind not born from blood, but from shared secrets, laughter, and silent understanding.

For many women, friendships become sacred spaces of refuge; a sisterhood of survival through heartbreaks, disappointments, and new beginnings. Yet even in friendship, there is often imbalance.

We are taught to be good friends: to show up, to listen, to forgive, to support. But what happens when the listener never gets to speak?

When the giver is never poured into? The truth is that many women carry friendships that demand their strength but rarely feed their soul. We confuse loyalty with obligation, mistaking emotional exhaustion for love.

Real friendship is not built on who gives the most; it's built on honesty, presence, and mutual respect.

But learning that lesson often comes through heartbreak, not betrayal; through the slow fading of something that once felt like home.

The Listener Who Lost Her Voice

Danielle was the friend everyone came to for advice. She had a calmness that made people feel safe, a heart so open that others poured their pain into it without hesitation.

Birthdays, breakups, crises; Danielle was there, always the first to show up and the last to be thanked.

But when her own life began to unravel, when her marriage ended and her job disappeared in the same month, her phone grew quiet.

The same people who once called her daily were nowhere to be found. She'd pick up the phone, scroll through her contacts, and realize she had no one to call who wouldn't say, "You're strong; you'll be fine."

She wasn't fine. She was empty. Years of being everyone's safe place had left her without one of her own.

One day, sitting alone on her porch, Danielle whispered to herself, "I've been the friend I needed, but I've never had her."

It was a painful truth; but also a freeing one. She stopped giving out pieces of herself to people who didn't notice when she was missing. Slowly, she began to rebuild her circle; smaller, quieter, but rooted in reciprocity. And for the first time, she learned that friendship should feel like rest, not responsibility.

The Friendship That Faded

For years, Mia and Jordan were inseparable. They met in college and stayed close through every milestone; marriages, babies, divorces, grief. They called each other "sisters by choice."

But somewhere along the way, life shifted.
Jordan's career took off while Mia's stalled. Conversations became strained; calls grew shorter.

Jordan began to speak more about her success, while Mia felt left behind; embarrassed, even, to share her struggles.

When Mia's mother passed away, Jordan sent flowers but didn't come to the funeral. "I couldn't get off work," she said later. The words sliced deeper than either of them expected.

 Months turned into years. And though both women loved each other, pride and pain built a quiet wall between them.

Then, one summer day, Mia received a handwritten note in the mail. It read, "I miss who we were before life made us careful." It was signed simply, "Love, Jordan."

It didn't fix everything. But it reminded them that sometimes, love in friendship isn't about staying the same, it's about forgiving who you've both become.

Friends for a Season

Not every friendship is meant to last forever, and one of the hardest lessons women learn is that love between friends can still be real even when the relationship no longer fits the season of life they are in.

As girls, friendships often feel simple. We bond over laughter, secrets, shared dreams, and the comfort of belonging. But adulthood changes the landscape of friendship. Marriage, children, careers, grief, divorce, financial differences, personal growth, and emotional healing all reshape the people we become.

Sometimes women grow together.

Sometimes they grow apart quietly.

And neither always means someone is wrong.

One friend may still crave closeness while the other is overwhelmed by survival. One woman may evolve emotionally while another remains emotionally unavailable. Some friendships weaken under jealousy, competition, or unspoken resentment. Others simply fade under the weight of time and responsibility.

The painful part is that many women mourn friendships silently because society rarely acknowledges friendship grief as real heartbreak. Yet losing a close friend can hurt just as deeply as losing a romantic relationship.

A good friend often knows:

your insecurities,

your history,

your family struggles,

your dreams,

and the version of you that existed before life hardened you.

When that bond changes, the loss leaves an emptiness dificult to explain.

The Friend Who Felt Left Behind

Nicole and Tasha had been inseparable since high school. They survived heartbreaks together, shared apartments in their twenties, and once promised they would grow old side by side. But life slowly pulled them into different worlds.

Nicole married, built a successful business, and traveled often. Tasha struggled financially after a dificult divorce and spent most of her energy trying to rebuild her life.

At first, they tried to stay close. But over time, the imbalance between them grew uncomfortable. Nicole talked excitedly about vacations and opportunities while Tasha quietly battled shame over how much her life had changed.

Neither woman intended to hurt the other. Yet every conversation began leaving Tasha emotionally exhausted.

Eventually, the calls became less frequent. Text messages turned into quick check-ins instead of real conversations.

One night, Tasha looked through old photographs of them laughing at twenty-three years old and cried unexpectedly. She realized she did not miss the activities they used to do — she missed feeling emotionally understood.

Years later, the women reunited briefly at a mutual friend's event. There was no anger between them. Only tenderness for what they once meant to each other.

Sometimes friendships do not end in betrayal.

Sometimes they simply end in distance.

And that can hurt just as much.

The Friend Who Carries Everyone
Many women become the emotional caretaker within their
friendships. They are the listeners, the encouragers, the
dependable ones who answer late-night phone calls and hold
space for everyone else's pain.
But women who constantly carry others often become experts
at hiding their own exhaustion.
They fear becoming "too much."
They fear burdening others.
So they continue giving even when emotionally depleted.
The world praises women for being nurturing, but very few
people ask nurturing women who is nurturing them.
Some women have spent decades being:
everyone's therapist,
everyone's support system,
everyone's safe place,
while secretly feeling unseen themselves.
And eventually, emotional burnout begins to look like
loneliness.

The Friendship That Couldn't Survive Growth
Andrea and Melissa built their friendship during dificult years.

Both women were struggling mothers trying to survive

financially and emotionally. Their friendship became a lifeline

during some of the hardest moments of their lives.

But as time passed, Andrea began changing. She started

therapy, returned to school, and slowly became more

confident. She learned boundaries, started saying no more

often, and became intentional about protecting her peace.

Melissa interpreted the changes as rejection.

"You think you're better than everybody now," she snapped

during an argument one afternoon.

Andrea was stunned because the truth was, she was finally

learning not to abandon herself for the comfort of others.

Their friendship slowly unraveled after that. Not because there

was no love left, but because growth changes relationships.

Sometimes when one woman heals, it forces others to confront

wounds they are not yet ready to face.

Andrea grieved the friendship deeply. But she also understood

something important:

not every relationship can survive the version of you that finally

chooses peace.

Friendship and Quiet Competition

One of the most uncomfortable truths about female friendships

is that comparison sometimes exists even where love does too.

Women are often conditioned to measure themselves against

one another:

- appearance,
- motherhood,
- marriage,
- finances,
- success,
- aging,
- relationships,
- happiness.

Sometimes competition enters friendships silently.

A friend may celebrate you publicly while privately struggling

with jealousy. Another may pull away when your life improves

because your progress reminds her of her own

disappointments.

This does not make women cruel.

It makes them human.

But healthy friendship requires emotional maturity — the ability to celebrate another woman's growth without seeing it as evidence of your own failure.

True friendship says:

"Your light does not take away from mine."

Learning to Release Friendships with Grace

Not every friendship is meant to be repaired. Some relationships served their purpose beautifully for a season and then naturally came to an end.

And that's okay.

Women often carry guilt when friendships fade, especially if there was no dramatic betrayal. But life changes people. Growth changes people. Pain changes people.

Releasing a friendship with grace means:

- honoring what it once was,
- accepting what it no longer is,
- and leting go without bitterness.

Some women spend years angry at friendships that simply outgrew themselves.

But healing begins when we stop asking:

"Why didn't it last forever?"

And begin asking:

"What did this friendship teach me about love, boundaries, loyalty, and myself?"

Every friendship leaves something behind:

wisdom,

comfort,

memory,

or growth.

Even the painful ones.

What This Season Teaches Us

Friendship is one of the first places women learn emotional intimacy outside of family. It teaches us how to trust, how to support, how to forgive, and sometimes, how to let go.

Some friends become lifelong sisters.

Others become beautiful chapters that eventually close.

Both relationships matter.

As women grow older, many begin valuing friendships differently. They stop chasing large circles and start craving emotional safety, honesty, peace, and reciprocity.

A mature friendship no longer requires performance. It becomes softer, steadier, and more understanding.

And perhaps the greatest lesson friendship teaches women is

this:

you should never have to abandon yourself in order to belong

to someone else.

The right friendships will not require you to shrink, compete,

over-give, or constantly prove your worth.

They will simply allow you to be fully seen —

and fully loved there.

The Friend: The One Who Listens but Is Rarely Heard

"Some friendships raise us, some drain us, and some quietly teach us who we are becoming."

Chapter 4: The Wife: Becoming What Love Demands

There is a quiet transformation that happens when a woman becomes a wife. It's not just the change of a name or the wearing of a ring, it's a shifting of identity, a soft surrender of independence wrapped in the promise of forever.

We grow up believing that marriage is the reward for love; the place where dreams find rest and partnership brings peace. But for many women, marriage becomes something more complicated: a test of endurance, a mirror of sacrifice, and sometimes, a slow fading of self in the name of devotion.

Being a wife teaches patience, forgiveness, and resilience; but it also reveals the parts of ourselves we gave away too freely, thinking it was love. Because love can make you bloom, but it can also make you forget your own fragrance when you spend too long watering everyone else.

The Woman Who Forgot Herself

Erica married young. She loved with all the innocence of someone who believed love alone could hold everything together.

Her husband was kind in the beginning, attentive, ambitious, and full of promises. But as the years passed, those promises became expectations, and Erica's world grew smaller.

She stopped going out with friends, stopped painting, stopped speaking up when she was hurt. Her life became a schedule of meals, bills, and responsibilities. She told herself this was what a good wife did; kept the peace, even when her heart was at war.

When her children left home, Erica realized she didn't know who she was anymore. Her husband still loved her, in his own quiet way, but she had forgotten how to love herself.

One night, she stood in front of the mirror and whispered, "I used to know the woman in this reflection. I wonder if she's still there."

Over time, Erica found her way back, through books, long walks, and the rediscovery of her voice. Her husband noticed the change, the spark returning. "You seem different," he said.

She smiled softly. "I'm becoming myself again."

Her story was not about leaving; it was about returning. Returning to the woman she was before she forgot that her needs mattered too.

The Woman Who Stayed Too Long

Melissa believed in love with every part of her being. She believed in vows, in commitment, in holding on. Even when her marriage turned cold, she stayed. Even when the laughter disappeared and the silence became unbearable, she told herself, "Good wives don't give up."

But good wives also shouldn't disappear.

Years went by, and Melissa became a ghost in her own home; managing, surviving, pretending. She stayed for the children, then for the memories, and finally, out of habit. Her friends stopped asking how she was. She stopped asking herself too.

It wasn't until one morning, siting across from her husband at breakfast, that she realized they hadn't looked at each other in years. He read the newspaper; she stared at her untouched coffee. She whispered under her breath, "I miss me."

That day, she didn't leave him. But she left the version of herself that settled for loneliness in the name of loyalty. She went back to school, joined a book club, and started living again, not as his wife, but as her own person.

When people asked if she was happy, she said,

"I'm healing — and that's enough."

When Love Demands Too Much

Marriage is not a fairy tale; it's a daily decision. A decision to listen, to forgive, to grow, and sometimes, to survive. But love should never cost you your identity. The vows we make are sacred, but so is the promise we owe ourselves: to remain whole.

Being a wife doesn't mean becoming invisible. It means learning how to love without losing your reflection in someone else's shadow.

Real love is not about endurance; it's about evolution. It's about two people growing side by side, not one person shrinking to make the other comfortable.

And when a woman remembers that her voice matters, her dreams matter, her peace matters, she becomes not just a wife, but a woman who loves from strength, not survival.

The Marriage Nobody Sees

There are marriages the world admires from the outside — the smiling photographs, holiday cards, anniversary dinners, shared routines, and carefully maintained image of stability. But behind many closed doors live women carrying loneliness no one else can see.

Not every unhappy marriage is loud.

Some are painfully quiet.

There are women who are not abused, not abandoned, and not unloved in obvious ways — yet still feel emotionally invisible. They share homes with men they no longer feel connected to. They discuss bills, children, schedules, and responsibilities while silently grieving the intimacy they once had.

This kind of loneliness is dificult to explain because nothing dramatic happened. Life simply became heavy. Responsibilities replaced romance. Exhaustion replaced curiosity. Survival replaced connection.

And slowly, the marriage became functional instead of emotional.

Many wives carry an invisible labor inside relationships:

- remembering birthdays,
- managing emotions,
- maintaining peace,
- anticipating needs,
- supporting dreams,
- holding families together.

Over time, some women become so consumed with taking care of everyone else that they stop asking themselves whether they feel emotionally cared for too.

The heartbreaking part is this:

many wives do not realize how empty they have become until the children are older, the house becomes quieter, and they finally have space to hear their own thoughts again.

The Woman Who Missed Her Own Laughter

Patricia used to laugh loudly when she was younger. Her friends described her as vibrant, funny, and full of life. But somewhere between marriage, motherhood, bills, and routine, that version of her slowly disappeared.

She didn't notice it all at once. It happened gradually:

she stopped dancing around the kitchen,

stopped calling friends as often,

stopped buying clothes she loved,

stopped doing small things that made her feel alive.

Her husband wasn't cruel. He worked hard and provided for the family. But emotionally, they had drifted into separate worlds. Their conversations became practical instead of personal.

One evening, while attending a family gathering, Patricia overheard someone laughing loudly across the room. The sound startled her because it reminded her of herself.

Or at least who she used to be.

Driving home that night, she stared out the car window quietly and thought:

"I cannot remember the last time I truly felt light."

That realization shook her deeply. Not because her marriage

had failed, but because somewhere inside it, she had

abandoned parts of herself she never intended to lose.

Healing for Patricia did not begin with leaving her marriage. It

began with reconnecting to herself again:

reading,

walking,

calling old friends,

allowing herself joy without guilt.

And little by little, her laughter returned.

The Emotional Labor of Wives

Many women are taught that love means giving endlessly.

So wives become emotional managers within their homes.

They monitor moods, smooth over conflict, carry invisible

stress, and often absorb everyone else's emotional needs while

suppressing their own.

The problem is that emotional labor is rarely acknowledged

because it is not always visible.

➢ No one sees:

➢ the mental exhaustion,

➢ the emotional planning,

> the constant caregiving,

the quiet pressure of holding relationships together.

And many wives become so skilled at managing everything that the people around them assume they are fine.

But strength without support eventually becomes burnout.

Some women spend years waiting to be emotionally noticed while silently carrying entire households on their backs.

And eventually, resentment grows where exhaustion is ignored too long.

The Wife Who Stayed Emotionally Lonely

Deborah had been married for twenty-seven years. From the outside, her life looked stable:

a nice home,

grown children,

vacations,

church every Sunday.

But privately, she often felt profoundly alone.

Her husband rarely asked how she was feeling. If she tried to talk about emotional distance, he would respond with practical solutions instead of connection. Over time, Deborah stopped bringing things up altogether.

She convinced herself this was simply what long marriages became.

One afternoon, while cleaning out old boxes, she found letters her husband had written while they were dating. The man in those letters sounded emotionally open, affectionate, curious, and attentive.

She sat on the floor crying because she realized she missed being emotionally pursued.

Not physically.

Emotionally.

That night, for the first time in years, she spoke honestly to her husband. Not angrily. Not dramatically. Just truthfully.

"I don't need perfection," she told him softly. "I just miss feeling emotionally close to you."

The conversation was uncomfortable. Healing did not happen overnight. But honesty reopened a door silence had kept closed for years.

Sometimes marriages do not need grand gestures.

Sometimes they simply need two people willing to stop pretending everything is fine.

Staying, Leaving, and Becoming

One of the most dificult decisions women face is determining

whether they are staying in a marriage from love or from fear:

fear of starting over,

fear of judgment,

fear of financial instability,

fear of loneliness,

fear of failing.

There is no simple answer because every marriage carries its

own history, wounds, and complexity.

Some women leave and rediscover themselves beautifully.

Some women stay and rebuild healthier relationships.

Some continue surviving emotionally disconnected lives

because they no longer know another way.

But regardless of the outcome, every woman deserves:

emotional safety,

respect,

partnership,

peace,

and the freedom to remain herself inside love.

Marriage should not require self-erasure as proof of

commitment.

When Women Begin Again

One of the most powerful moments in a woman's life happens when she stops waiting for permission to reclaim herself.

She remembers:

- what brings her joy,
- what makes her feel alive,
- what dreams she postponed,
- and what parts of herself still deserve attention.

Some women rediscover themselves inside marriage.

Others rediscover themselves after it.

But either way, healing begins when a woman realizes she matters too.

Not only as:

- a wife,
- a mother,
- a caretaker,
- or a supporter—

but as a complete human being with needs, desires, dreams, and emotional depth of her own.

What This Season Teaches Us

Marriage teaches women some of life's deepest lessons about intimacy, sacrifice, identity, disappointment, forgiveness, and emotional resilience.

It reveals:

- how people change,

- how love evolves,

- and how easy it is to lose yourself while trying to hold everything together.

But healthy love should never require a woman to disappear emotionally in order to maintain peace.

The strongest marriages are not built on perfection. They are built on honesty, growth, mutual care, and the willingness to keep seeing one another fully even after years together.

And perhaps the most important lesson this season teaches is this:

a woman should never have to choose between being loved and being herself.

The Wife: Becoming What Love Demands

"Some women lose themselves so quietly inside marriage that even they do not notice they are disappearing."

Chapter 5: The Mother: When Love Isn't Enough

Motherhood changes everything.

It is the one role that defines a woman in the eyes of others more than any other. It's a title wrapped in pride, fear, sleepless nights, and endless hope.

We are told it's the purest love we'll ever know, and it is. But no one warns you that sometimes, even the deepest love cannot protect your child from life's hardest lessons... or from themselves.

There's a secret ache that only mothers understand; the fear that your child's choices will reflect your failures. That somewhere, somehow, you went wrong.

And when that fear comes true, when your child becomes the one you can no longer reach, it cuts deeper than any heartbreak love has ever known.

The Son She Couldn't Save

Tanya was a single mother who gave her son everything she could. She worked two jobs, skipped meals, and prayed every night for his future. "You're my reason for everything," she'd tell him.

He grew up loved, but restless. By his late teens, he drifted into a crowd that promised him belonging.

Tanya begged, pleaded, threatened, prayed; but the streets spoke louder than she could.

One night, the phone rang. A call no mother ever wants to receive. Her son had been arrested.

Tanya's heart broke, not just from what happened, but from the cruel thought that whispered in her mind: Where did I fail?
At the courthouse, she sat quietly, clutching his childhood photo in her hand. She looked at him, older now, angry, lost, and whispered, "I still love you. Even here."

Years later, when he was released, he told her, "You never gave up on me. I just didn't know how to let you in."

That moment didn't erase the pain, but it brought healing; the kind born from unconditional love that refuses to disappear even when the story doesn't end the way we dreamed.

The Daughter Who Chose Distance

For years, Carla and her daughter Jasmine were inseparable. They shared everything, long talks, late-night laughter, and dreams for the future.

But as Jasmine grew older, the bond began to fray. What once was closeness turned into criticism, misunderstandings, and hurt that neither could fix.

Carla tried to hold on. She sent texts, wrote letters, and left voicemails. The silence that followed became unbearable. Her daughter had built walls that love alone couldn't break.

One Christmas, Carla mailed a card that simply said, "No matter how far you go, my love follows you." She didn't expect a response, but months later, one came.

It was a short message: "I needed time to find myself, not away from you, but because of you."

Carla cried for hours not because the pain had vanished, but because she finally understood sometimes love means stepping back, even when it breaks your heart.

When Love Hurts More Than It Heals Mothers often measure their worth through their children's success or happiness. But the truth is, motherhood is not about perfection; it's about presence. It's about showing up, even when your heart is shattered.

There are no guarantees in parenting. You can give your best and still face heartbreak. You can pour love into a child and watch them walk into darkness anyway.

But your love is not wasted. It becomes a light, maybe not one they follow immediately, but one that never burns out.
When love isn't enough, faith must be. Faith that one day, your child will remember the warmth of your hands, the sound of your prayers, and the truth that they were always loved beyond measure.

And even when a mother's heart breaks, it still beats; because a mother's love is the only love that survives even in silence.

The Weight Mothers Never Put Down

There is no role that changes a woman more completely than motherhood. The moment a child enters her life, whether through birth, adoption, or circumstance, something inside her shifts forever. Her heart no longer belongs only to her. It begins walking around outside her body in the form of another human being.

And from that moment forward, a mother worries.

She worries when her children are small:

- Are they safe?
- Are they healthy?
- Am I doing enough?

Then they grow older, and the worries simply change shape:

Are they making good choices?

Are they emotionally okay?

Did I prepare them well enough for life?

Motherhood is filled with invisible emotional labor that rarely ends, even after children become adults.

A mother can be:

- exhausted,
- overwhelmed,
- financially stressed,

- emotionally drained,

  and still somehow continue showing up because love

  keeps pushing her forward even when her body and

  spirit are tired.

What many women never admit out loud is this:

motherhood often comes with guilt no matter how hard you

try.

If you work too much, you feel guilty.

If you rest, you feel guilty.

If your child struggles, you blame yourself.

If your child succeeds, you quietly wonder whether you

deserved any credit at all.

Many mothers spend years believing they are only as successful

as their children appear to be.

And that emotional burden can become unbearable.

The Mother Who Did Everything Right

Janice did everything she believed a good mother was

supposed to do. She attended school events, helped with

homework, prayed over her children every night, and sacrificed

constantly so they could have opportunities she never had

growing up.

Her son Marcus was intelligent, kind, and full of promise as a child. But somewhere during his teenage years, anger began taking hold of him. He became distant, rebellious, and eventually involved with drugs.

Janice blamed herself immediately.

She replayed every parenting decision in her mind:

- Was I too strict?

- Too soft?

- Did I miss warning signs?

- Did I fail him somehow?

The guilt consumed her quietly. She stopped sharing her struggles openly because she feared judgment from others. Mothers often feel ashamed when their children's lives do not unfold the way they hoped.

One night, after another painful argument with her son, Janice sat on her bedroom floor crying and whispered:

"I gave him everything I had. Why wasn't it enough?"

The truth was devastating but important:

sometimes love cannot prevent every wound life brings.

Parents can guide, teach, support, pray, and sacrifice — but children eventually become individuals with their own choices, pain, and journeys.

Janice slowly learned that loving her son did not mean controlling his path. It meant refusing to stop loving him even while grieving the direction his life had taken.

Mothers and Silent Comparison

One of the cruelest emotional traps mothers fall into is comparison.

Women constantly compare themselves:

- whose children behave better,

- whose child graduated first,

- whose daughter became successful,

- whose son stayed out of trouble,

- whose family appears happier.

Social media has only deepened this emotional pressure.

Mothers scroll through polished family photos while privately feeling like they are failing behind closed doors.

But every family carries hidden struggles.

Some mothers smile publicly while privately:

- praying over addicted children,

- worrying about mental health struggles,

- grieving broken relationships,

- or carrying deep exhaustion no one else sees.

Motherhood was never meant to be a performance competition.

Yet many women spend years measuring themselves against unrealistic expectations instead of offering themselves compassion.

The Empty Nest That Felt Like Grief

Sandra spent most of her adult life raising children. Her entire routine revolved around motherhood:

school schedules,

sports practices,

doctor appointments,

college applications,

family dinners.

Then suddenly, the house became quiet.

Her youngest daughter left for college, and for the first time in over twenty years, Sandra sat alone in a silent kitchen unsure what to do next.

Everyone congratulated her:

"You finally get time for yourself!"

But nobody prepared her for the grief.

Because motherhood had not simply been something she did — it had become who she was.

Without the constant responsibilities, Sandra realized she no longer knew what brought her joy personally.

One afternoon, she wandered through a bookstore and unexpectedly burst into tears reading a simple sentence in a novel:

"She had spent so many years raising everyone else that she forgot she was still growing too."

That sentence changed something inside her.

Slowly, Sandra began rediscovering herself:

- taking art classes,
- traveling with friends,
- volunteering,
- learning to exist beyond constant caregiving.

She still loved her children deeply. But she was finally learning this truth:

motherhood is a chapter of a woman's identity — not the entire book.

Loving Children Through Disappointment

One of the deepest pains mothers carry is loving children who hurt them.

Sometimes the pain comes through:

- addiction,

- emotional distance,

- disrespect,

- poor life choices,

- rejection,

- or years of unresolved conflict.

And yet, mothers continue loving anyway.

A mother's love is complicated because it rarely disappears, even after disappointment. Many women continue praying for children who no longer call them, worrying about children who reject their advice, and hoping for reconciliation long after others would have given up.

This kind of love can feel both beautiful and heartbreaking at the same time.

Some mothers quietly carry grief for relationships with children that never became what they hoped.

And still, they love.

Because motherhood teaches women something profound: love is not always measured by outcomes. Sometimes it is measured by endurance.

Mothers Are Human Too

Society often treats mothers as though they should be endlessly patient, nurturing, selfless, and emotionally available at all times. But mothers are human beings before they are anything else.

They get tired.

They become discouraged.

They make mistakes.

They sometimes lose themselves under the weight of everyone else's needs.

And many women spend years denying their own emotional needs because they believe motherhood requires total self-sacrifice.

But children do not benefit from mothers who completely disappear inside caregiving.

Children also need to witness:

- healthy boundaries,

- self-respect,

- joy,

- healing,

- and emotional honesty.

One of the greatest gifts a mother can give her children is showing them that women deserve care too.

What This Season Teaches Us

Motherhood teaches women the deepest forms of love, fear, sacrifice, vulnerability, and resilience they may ever experience.

It teaches us:

- how fiercely the heart can love,

- how deeply it can ache,

- and how powerful unconditional love truly is.

But motherhood also teaches women something equally important:

you cannot measure your worth only by the choices your children make.

Children are not proof of perfection or failure. They are human beings navigating life just like their parents once did.

A mother's love matters even when outcomes are imperfect.

Even when relationships become strained.

Even when children lose their way.

And perhaps the greatest lesson motherhood teaches is this:
love does not always fix everything — but it leaves a light
behind that never fully goes out.

The Mother: When Love Isn't Enough

"A mother carries her children twice — first in her body, and then in her heart for the rest of her life."

Chapter 6: The Single Parent: Carrying the World Alone

There's a kind of strength the world doesn't see, the kind that gets up every morning when your body aches, when your spirit trembles, and when there's no one to share the weight.

Being a single parent is not just a role; it's a constant act of bravery. It's the art of holding it all together with hands that never truly rest.

The single mother, the single father, they live in a rhythm of sacrifice. They become both nurturer and provider, comforter and disciplinarian, the voice of reason and the shoulder to cry on. The world calls them strong, but strength wasn't a choice; it was a necessity.

And yet, behind every strong single parent is a heart that whispers in the quiet hours, "How much longer can I keep doing this?"

The Woman Who Became the Anchor When Angela's marriage ended, her son was only three. She had no savings, no child support, and no family nearby.

What she did have was a fierce determination that her child would never feel unloved, no matter how hard it got.

Days blurred into nights filled with double shifts and fast-food dinners. Some mornings, she'd wake up still in her work clothes, praying her son wouldn't see the exhaustion in her eyes. She smiled for him even when she was breaking.

When he asked one night, "Mom, are we poor?" she replied softly, "No, baby — we're blessed and brave."

Years later, at his high school graduation, her son gave his speech and said, "My mother taught me that strength doesn't roar, sometimes it just whispers, 'keep going.'" Angela cried quietly in the back row. All the long nights, the loneliness, the tears; they hadn't been in vain. Her love had built a life, one small sacrifice at a time.

The Father Who Chose to Stay

Not every single parent story belongs to a mother, some belong to fathers who refused to walk away.

When Jerome's wife passed unexpectedly, he became both mother and father to their two daughters. He didn't know how to braid hair or attend parent-teacher meetings without her, but he learned.

He learned to sit through dance recitals, cook pancakes on Saturday mornings, and listen to teenage heartbreaks.

He also learned about grief; how it lingers quietly even when you keep moving. Late at night, he'd stand in the hallway, watching his daughters sleep, wondering if he was enough.

Years later, when his oldest left for college, she wrote him a note: "You were never just enough,
Dad. You were everything."

Jerome folded that note and carried it in his wallet for the rest of his life.

The Weight and the Wonder

Being a single parent means carrying both the burden and the beauty of two hearts. It's living without a safety net, learning to celebrate alone, and finding joy in the smallest victories, like keeping the lights on or hearing your child say, "I love you."

It's also about learning to forgive yourself; for being tired, for not having enough, for breaking down behind closed doors. Because love doesn't require perfection. It requires presence.

Single parents are the unsung heroes of everyday life. They are proof that love can rebuild what loss has taken. They show their children not just how to survive, but how to rise; how to stand strong even when the world doesn't see the storm they're standing in.

So to the single parent; the one still pushing through long nights and lonely mornings; know this: your love is enough. Your efforts are enough. And you, even when unseen, are enough.

The Exhaustion of Being Everything

There is a level of exhaustion single parents carry that is dificult to explain to people who have never lived it. It is not just physical tiredness — it is emotional fatigue, mental overload, financial pressure, and the constant awareness that there is rarely anyone else to catch you if you fall.

Single parents become:

- providers,
- protectors,
- nurturers,
- disciplinarians,
- chauffeurs,
- counselors,
- and emotional anchors all at once.

And most of the time, they do it while carrying private fear nobody else fully sees.

There are no breaks from responsibility when children depend entirely on you. Even rest comes with guilt because there is always something left undone:

- bills to pay,
- groceries to buy,
- school meetings,

- emotional conversations,

- unexpected emergencies.

Many single parents live in a constant state of survival while smiling publicly so their children feel secure.

The world often praises single parents for being "strong," but few people stop to ask what that strength is costing them emotionally.

Because strength without support can slowly become loneliness.

Crying in the Grocery Store

Danielle stood in the grocery aisle staring at the price of eggs while mentally calculating what she could put back. Her two children were laughing nearby, unaware of the panic rising in her chest.

She had worked overtime all week, skipped meals herself several times, and still felt like she was falling behind financially.

The hardest part was not the money.

It was the fear.

The fear of not being enough.

The fear of failing quietly while everyone assumed she was managing fine.

Danielle grabbed the cart tightly and forced herself not to cry until she reached the parking lot. Once inside the car, she broke down completely.

Not because of groceries.

Because she was tired of carrying everything alone.

After a few minutes, she wiped her tears before her children climbed into the car. Then she smiled and asked what they wanted for dinner.

This is the hidden reality many single parents live every day: breaking privately while holding everything together publicly.

The Loneliness Nobody Talks About

Single parenting can feel emotionally isolating, even when surrounded by people.

Friends may sympathize, but many cannot fully understand the mental load:

- making every major decision alone,
- worrying alone,
- recovering from setbacks alone,
- carrying the emotional atmosphere of the household alone.

At night, after the children are asleep, the silence often feels heavier. That is when the fears become louder:

- What if something happens to me?
- Am I ruining my children somehow?
- Will I ever stop feeling this overwhelmed?
- Who takes care of me?

Some single parents become so focused on survival that they stop viewing themselves as individuals with emotional needs. Their identity becomes entirely wrapped around responsibility. And over time, many quietly lose connection with:

- friendships,
- hobbies,
- dreams,
- romance,
- and even joy.

Not because they no longer desire those things — but because survival consumes all available energy.

Learning to Ask for Help

Tamika hated asking for help.

After her divorce, she became determined to prove she could handle everything herself. She worked full-time, attended every school event, paid every bill she could manage, and refused to let anyone see her struggle.

But eventually, the pressure became overwhelming. She was exhausted constantly, emotionally drained, and becoming impatient with her children over small things.

One evening, after forgeting a school project deadline, her son looked at her sadly and said:

"It's okay, Mom. I know you're trying."

That sentence broke her.

Because for the first time, she realized her children were noticing her exhaustion too.

The next week, Tamika called her sister and asked for help with after-school pickups twice a week. It felt uncomfortable at first because she viewed needing help as weakness.

But slowly, she began learning something important:

support does not make you incapable.

It makes you human.

Single parents often carry shame around needing assistance because society glorifies independence. But no one was meant to raise children entirely alone without emotional support. Healing began for Tamika the moment she stopped trying to prove she could survive without help and started allowing herself to receive care too.

Dating, Loneliness, and Starting Again

One of the most complicated emotional experiences for single parents is learning how to balance personal desires with parental responsibilities.

Many single mothers and fathers feel guilty even thinking about romance again. They worry:

- about introducing someone new into their children's lives,

- about being judged,

- about repeating painful mistakes,

- or about whether they even remember how to love anymore.

Some remain emotionally closed off for years because survival leaves little room for vulnerability. Others settle for unhealthy relationships simply because loneliness becomes overwhelming.

But loneliness can make people ignore warning signs they would normally recognize clearly.

Single parents often crave partnership not because they are weak, but because they are tired of carrying life alone.

There is nothing selfish about wanting companionship, support, tenderness, or emotional connection after years of struggle.

The challenge is learning how to seek love without abandoning the peace and stability you fought so hard to build.

When the Children Become the Motivation

Many single parents survive impossible seasons because their children become the reason they keep going.

There are parents who:

- worked multiple jobs,

- skipped meals,

- postponed dreams,

- stayed awake worrying,

- cried silently at night,

  while still showing up every morning because someone small was depending on them.

Children may never fully understand the sacrifices their parents made while they were growing up. But love leaves evidence over time:

in stability,

in safety,

in emotional presence,

in resilience,

and in the lessons children carry into adulthood.

Single parents often underestimate the impact of simply continuing to show up despite exhaustion.

Sometimes survival itself becomes an act of love.

What This Season Teaches Us

Single parenting teaches women and men some of life's hardest lessons about endurance, sacrifice, humility, resilience, and emotional strength.

It reveals:

- how strong people can become under pressure,
- how loneliness changes a person,
- and how deeply love motivates survival.

But it also teaches something equally important: strength should not require total isolation.

No one was meant to carry life completely alone.

Single parents deserve:

- support,

- rest,

- emotional care,

- understanding,

- and moments of peace too.

And perhaps the greatest lesson this season teaches is this:

being overwhelmed does not mean you are failing.

Sometimes the strongest people are simply the ones who kept

going despite how heavy everything felt.

The Single Parent: Carrying the World Alone

"Single parents learn how to survive exhaustion while still pretending everything is under control."

Chapter 7: The Grandmother: Lessons in Grace

There is a gentleness that comes with age; a slowing of pace, a quiet knowing that not everything in life needs to be fixed to be understood.

A grandmother carries more than wrinkles and memories; she carries generations of stories, sacrifices, and lessons etched into her heart.

She has seen love in all its forms; the joy of it, the ache of it, the parts that survive long after the heart breaks.

She has lived through mistakes that became lessons, and lessons that became wisdom. And now, she watches her children and grandchildren live their own versions of the same stories she once thought were unique to her.

Being a grandmother is not just about baking cookies or offering comfort; it's about grace.
The kind that no longer seeks to control, but to understand. The kind that lets go of judgment and embraces forgiveness. The kind that loves freely, without needing to be right.

The Healing of Distance

Margaret had not spoken to her daughter in nearly ten years. Their relationship had fractured over choices made in youth; harsh words, misunderstood intentions, and pride that stood taller than love.

When her daughter had children of her own, Margaret longed to be part of their lives, but the past stood in the way. She sent cards every year, gifts that were returned unopened.

Then one Christmas, there was a knock on her door. When she opened it, her daughter stood there, tears streaming down her face, holding a small boy's hand.

"Mom," she whispered, "this is your grandson." In that moment, words weren't needed. They fell into each other's arms; not as mother and daughter bound by guilt, but as women who finally understood that love had always been the goal, even when pride got in the way.

Later that night, as Margaret rocked her grandson to sleep, she realized that forgiveness is not about forgetting the past; it's about refusing to let it ruin what's still possible.

The Keeper of the Family Flame

Evelyn had raised four children alone. Now in her seventies, she was the heartbeat of her family; the one everyone called, the one who prayed for them all, the one whose kitchen felt like home.

Her grandchildren saw her as a pillar of strength, but what they didn't know was how often she'd cried in secret through the years.

Every generation had its own chaos, its own wounds, but Evelyn never stopped believing that love could hold them together.

At her eightieth birthday celebration, her oldest grandson stood up to speak. "Our grandmother taught us what love looks like in motion," he said. "She loved us when we were easy to love, and when we weren't. She forgave when others gave up. She held us even when we pushed her away."

Evelyn smiled through tears, realizing she had done something no one had taught her to do, she had broken the cycle of bitterness. Through every hardship, she had chosen grace over resentment, love over pride.

That was her legacy.

The Wisdom of Grace

Grandmothers carry time differently. They see the world through eyes that have wept and healed, through hands that have built and released, through hearts that have broken and mended more times than anyone knows.

Their wisdom doesn't come from perfection; it comes from endurance. From learning that love does not always come easy, but it always comes back when given freely.

A grandmother's grace is a soft reminder to the next generation:

Don't let pride steal your peace.

Don't let time pass without forgiveness.

And don't forget that family, though imperfect, is the soil from which your strength grows.

Because when all is said and done, it's not the things she owned or the advice she gave that her family would remember; it's the way she loved them through it all.

Watching Time Repeat Itself

One of the strangest parts of growing older is watching younger generations repeat the same mistakes you once made yourself. Grandmothers often see life differently because time has softened certain illusions. They understand:

- how quickly years pass,
- how pride damages relationships,
- how important forgiveness becomes,
- and how little material things matter in the end.

There is both wisdom and helplessness in this stage of life. Many grandmothers watch their children and grandchildren struggle with:

- relationships,
- financial hardship,
- parenting,
- identity,
- heartbreak,
- and poor choices.

And while they may recognize the warning signs immediately, they also understand something painful:

people often must learn certain lessons through experience.

That realization can be dificult.

Grandmothers want to protect the people they love, but age teaches restraint. They learn when to speak, when to stay silent, and when to simply offer love without control.
This kind of wisdom only comes through living.

Raising Children Again

Loretta thought her years of active parenting were behind her.
Her children were grown, she had finally retired, and for the first time in decades, life had become quieter.
Then her daughter began struggling with addiction.
Within months, Loretta found herself raising her two young grandchildren full-time. School drop-offs, homework, doctor visits, sleepless nights — everything she thought she had already completed in life suddenly returned.
At first, she felt angry privately. Not at her grandchildren, but at the exhaustion of starting over at an age when her body was already tired.
One night, while folding tiny clothes again after midnight, Loretta sat quietly and cried.
Not because she regretted helping.
But because she never imagined this would become her story.

Still, every morning she woke up and kept going because love demanded it.

Years later, her grandson stood at his high school graduation and publicly thanked her:

"You gave me stability when everything else was falling apart."

In that moment, Loretta realized something powerful: sometimes grandmothers become the bridge that keeps a family from completely breaking apart.

Grandmothers Become Family Historians

As women age, they often become the emotional memory keepers of the family.

Grandmothers remember:

where everyone came from,

who sacrificed what,

who struggled silently,

who loved deeply,

and how the family survived dificult seasons together.

They carry stories younger generations may never fully understand until much later in life.

A grandmother's kitchen often becomes more than a room. It becomes:

a safe place,

a counseling ofice,

a prayer room,

a gathering place,

and sometimes the only emotional stability within a fractured family.

Many grandmothers quietly hold families together through presence alone.

Children and grandchildren often feel safest with them because grandmothers love differently than parents do. Time softens expectations. Their love becomes less about control and more about understanding.

Grandmothers know life is dificult. They no longer expect perfection.

They simply want connection before time runs out.

The Grandmother Who Chose Peace

Eleanor spent most of her younger years arguing constantly with family members. She was outspoken, controlling, and deeply opinionated. She believed keeping everyone together meant correcting everyone constantly.

But after losing her husband unexpectedly in her sixties, something inside her changed.

Grief softened her.

She realized how much energy she had wasted trying to win arguments that no longer mattered. So she made a quiet decision:

she wanted peace more than control.

Over time, her relationships with her children improved dramatically. They called more often, visited longer, and trusted her emotionally in ways they never had before.

One afternoon, her granddaughter asked:

"Grandma, how did you become so calm?"

Eleanor smiled softly and answered:

"Because life taught me love matters more than being right."

That wisdom became one of the greatest gifts she passed down to her family.

Not perfection.

Not money.

Peace.

The Tenderness That Comes with Age

Many women become gentler with themselves as they grow older.

The things that once consumed them:

- appearance,

- competition,

- proving themselves,

- perfection,
begin losing importance.

Grandmothers understand something younger women are still
learning:
life is fragile,
time moves quickly,
and emotional peace is priceless.

This does not mean older women stop hurting. In fact, many carry
enormous grief:

- loss of spouses,

- declining health,

- loneliness,

- fractured family relationships,

- or regret over time wasted.

But aging often creates emotional clarity too.

Women begin seeing themselves with more compassion. They stop expecting perfection and start valuing presence, peace, and authenticity instead.

There is beauty in that softness.

Legacy Is More Than Money

Many grandmothers worry about what they will leave behind. But legacy is rarely just financial.

A woman's greatest legacy often becomes:

- the love she gave,

- the emotional safety she created,

- the wisdom she shared,

- the forgiveness she modeled,

- and the resilience she passed down through generations.

Long after material things disappear, families remember:

- how she made them feel,

- how she comforted them,

- how she survived dificult seasons,

- and how she loved despite hardship.

Grandmothers teach families that strength and gentleness can exist together.

And often, they become living proof that survival does not harden everyone. Some people become softer because of what they endured.

What This Season Teaches Us

Grandmotherhood teaches women some of life's final and most meaningful lessons about grace, perspective, forgiveness, and legacy.

It teaches us:

- that time is precious,
- that relationships matter deeply,
- and that emotional peace becomes more valuable than pride.

This season reminds women that wisdom is not about having lived perfectly. It is about surviving honestly and loving anyway.

Grandmothers carry generations inside them:

their childhood memories,

their motherhood journeys,

their heartbreaks,

their endurance,

their healing.

And perhaps the greatest lesson this season teaches is this:

a woman's life cannot be measured only by what she achieved materially.

Sometimes her greatest success is simply this:

through every hardship life placed before her, she continued choosing love.

The Grandmother: Lessons in Grace

"Grandmothers become the quiet keepers of memory, carrying stories the rest of the family has forgotten."

Chapter 8: The Woman Herself: Who Are You Now?

There comes a moment in every woman's life when the world grows quiet; the children are grown, the house no longer echoes with laughter, and the responsibilities that once consumed her begin to fade.

She sits with herself, perhaps for the first time in decades, and asks the question she's avoided all her life:

Who am I now?

For so many years, her identity was tied to what she did for others.

She was someone's **daughter.**

Someone's **sister.**

Someone's **best friend.**

Someone's **wife.**

Someone's **mother.**

Someone's **grandmother.**

Every chapter of her life was written for someone else. And now, in the quiet of her own company, she begins to see the outline of the woman beneath all those roles; the one who loved deeply, fell hard, got back up, and kept giving even when she had nothing left to give.

This is the rediscovery; not of who she was, but of who she has become.

The Woman Who Chose Herself at Last

Denise was seventy when she booked her first solo trip.
Her children thought she'd lost her mind, "Mom, what if something happens to you?" they asked. She smiled gently and said, "Something already did. I forgot how to live."

For most of her life, Denise had played it safe, following rules, meeting expectations, living responsibly. But after her husband's passing, she realized she had spent more years existing for others than truly living for herself.

So, she went to Italy; a place she'd always dreamed of but never dared to visit. She wandered through small towns, ate alone in cafés, watched sunsets from quiet rooftops, and rediscovered laughter that didn't depend on anyone else's company.

When she returned home, her daughter asked,

"Did you find what you were looking for?"

Denise smiled and said, "Yes. I found me."

The Woman Who Made Peace with Her Reflection Marjorie had spent a lifetime carrying guilt; guilt for things she couldn't change, for words left unsaid, for dreams she'd put away so others could chase theirs. She often stood in front of her mirror, seeing not herself, but all the versions of who she used to be.

One morning, she decided to do something different. She lit a candle, looked into her reflection, and whispered, "I forgive you."

It was such a simple act, but in that moment, years of self-blame began to loosen their grip. She no longer saw herself as the sum of her mistakes — but as a survivor of them.

Marjorie realized she didn't need to start over; she only needed to begin again; this time, with gentleness.

That day, she began to paint again, write again, laugh again. Her life wasn't perfect; but it finally felt like hers.

Becoming the Woman You Were Always Meant to Be

The final phase of womanhood isn't about age; it's about awakening. It's when we stop chasing what we were taught to be and start embracing who we truly are.

This woman no longer seeks validation. She no longer apologizes for her dreams, her silence, her choices, or her peace.

She knows that worth isn't proven; it's lived.

She carries every version of herself inside her, the daughter who obeyed, the sister who cared, the friend who listened, the wife who sacrificed, the mother who endured, the grandmother who forgave.

But now, she lives for the woman who remained when everyone else's needs were met, the woman who still dreams, still learns, still loves, and still hopes.

Because the journey of womanhood was never about becoming everything to everyone; it was always about finding your way back to yourself. And when she finally does, she realizes something powerful:

She was never lost. She was simply waiting for her own permission to begin again.

Womanhood is not a straight path; it's a winding road filled with tears, laughter, sacrifice, and rebirth. Every phase teaches us something vital: that love is both a gift and a lesson, that endurance can coexist with softness, and that even through heartbreak, we continue to rise.

From the daughter who tried her best to please, to the sister who held a family together, to the friend who poured from an empty cup to the wife who loved beyond measure, to the mother who carried both joy and sorrow, to the grandmother who learned forgiveness, and finally, to the woman herself; this is not just our story. It is every woman's story.

We may stumble, we may lose ourselves, but we always find our way back; wiser, stronger, and more at peace.
Because in the end, womanhood is not about who we became for others; it's about who we found when everything else fell away.
 May every reader see herself somewhere in these pages and know:

 You are not alone. You are becoming. You are already enough.

I wrote this book because I've lived every chapter of it in one way or another; as a daughter who carried her mother's expectations, as a friend who listened more than she spoke, as a wife who lost herself in love, as a mother who prayed through sleepless nights, and as a woman who finally sat still long enough to meet herself again.

This book is a reflection of the quiet pain women carry and the unspoken courage it takes to keep showing up.

I wanted to give voice to the women who feel unseen; the single mothers holding their families together, the grandmothers who carry generations of wisdom, the wives who wonder when love became duty, and the women who are rediscovering themselves after everyone else's needs were met.

I wrote this book as a gentle reminder: Your life has meaning even in the moments that broke you.

You are not defined by your mistakes, but by your ability to keep going.

And no matter what season of womanhood you are in; there is still time to begin again.

If this book touched your heart and you are ready to continue your personal journey of healing and self-discovery, here are a few resources that may support you:

Books by Vgdawson

I Need to Think About My Life Choices

Friends for Life: How to Grow and Keep Friendships for a Lifetime

After the Love Is Gone: Finding Strength in a Loveless Relationship

Dear Self: Reflections and Resilience Across Life's Journey

When Grace Looks Like Goodbye

Support and Self-Care Practices Create small daily rituals of stillness — journaling, prayer, or reflection.

Seek therapy or support groups when your emotional load feels heavy.

Surround yourself with friends who listen, not just talk.

Remember: healing isn't linear, but it is possible.

Leave a Review

If this book moved you, inspired you, or made you see your story differently, I would be deeply grateful if you left a review.

Your words not only help others discover this message — they remind me that stories of truth and vulnerability still matter.

Please take a moment to share your thoughts on:
Amazon | Goodreads | Barnes & Noble

Every review is a voice of encouragement that keeps independent authors like me writing stories that heal hearts.

Let's continue this journey together. I'd love to hear your
thoughts, stories, or reflections about how this book spoke to you.

Connect with vgdawson:

Website: www.what2buynext.com

Email: what2buynext2@outlook.com

Instagram: @what2buynext

Literary Candle Collection: Vgdawson Literary
Candles (inspired by my books)

Your voice matters to me. Stay connected,
because every story, including yours, deserves to be heard.

Courage Begins Where Fear Lives

A Guide to Finding Strength
Beyond Fear

Vgdawson

Courage Begins Where Fear Lives is a powerful reminder that fear does not disqualify you—it invites you.

In a world filled with uncertainty, pressure, and constant comparison, courage is often misunderstood. It isn't about being fearless or having all the answers. True courage is quieter. It's the steady choice to move forward honestly, even when fear is present.

This book explores courage as a daily practice—one rooted in self-trust, strength, mindset, persistence, growth, and meaning. Through reflective insights and practical guidance, readers are invited to rethink fear, reconnect with their inner strength, and choose themselves with intention.

Author of books on relationships, personal growth, and life transitions.

Stop Regreting the Past and
Start Designing a Life You
Love

Vgdawson

So many women spend years apologizing
for the past, replaying old wounds, and
carrying regret for choices they made
when they didn't know better. But here is
the truth: your past is not a life sentence.

WHAT YOU DON'T CHANGE, YOU CHOOSE

*Stop Regretting the Past
and Start Designing a Life You Love*

by vgdawson

What You Don't Change, You Choose is a powerful, heart centered guide for
women who have survived, sacrificed, stayed too long, and are finally ready to
stop living in regret and start living on purpose.

With honesty, compassion, and lived wisdom, author vgdawson walks you
through the defining moments, wasted years, and silent choices that shaped
your life— then shows you how to reclaim your power and choose differently.

Author of books on relationships, personal growth, and life transitions.

I Need to Think About My Life Choices

We don't always know when we're at a crossroads

Vgdawson

A Journal for Reflecting on Life Choices" is a transformative self-help journal designed to guide you through a thoughtful and introspective journey. This journal encourages you to reflect on your life choices, fostering a deeper understanding of your decisions and their impact on your life.

Through engaging prompts and insightful questions, "I Need to Think" helps you explore your inner thoughts, clarify your goals, and cultivate a more meaningful and purposeful life. Dive into this journal to challenge your thinking patterns, reshape your mindset, and embark on a path of self-discovery and personal growth. This is the first in a series of journals dedicated to helping you live your best life.

Author of books on relationships, personal growth, and life transitions.

The Friendship Year

A Season for Every Bond

Vgdawson

The Friendship Year: A Season for Every Bond is your essential field guide to the beautiful, messy, and vital world of friendship. Using the timeless metaphor of the seasons, this heartfelt book provides a compassionate framework for understanding every phase of connection.

Blending real, relatable stories with thoughtful insights and gentle humor, this book is a learning tool for the heart. It validates the grief of a friendship ended, celebrates the resilience of a bond renewed, and offers a language for the love that often goes unspoken.

If you've ever felt confused by a friend's distance, grateful for a friend's quiet support, or wondered how to be a better friend yourself, this book is for you. It's a warm, wise companion that proves you're not alone in navigating the most important map of all: the map of the heart.

Author of books on relationships, personal growth, and life transitions.

Thank You

To every woman who picked up this book — thank you.
Thank you for seeing yourself in these pages, for allowing my
words to touch the tender parts of your story, and for walking
with me through the many phases of womanhood.

Thank you to every daughter trying her best, every mother doing
what she can, every wife who stayed longer than she should,
every friend who kept showing up, and every grandmother who
carries love through generations. And most of all, thank you to
you — the woman reading this now, who keeps finding courage in
her own becoming.
This book was written for you.

May you never forget you are the story, the lesson, and the light.
With all my heart,

Vgdawson

BECOMING HER

www.ingramcontent.com/pod-product-compliance
Lightning Source LLC
Chambersburg PA
CBHW050951050726
47592CB00007B/2517